A Guide to the
FAVOURITE WATERFALLS
OF
PERTHSHIRE

by
David Watson

First published in 2010 by
Photoprint Scotland

© David & Rosemary Watson
watson.dr@btinternet.com

ISBN 978-0-9559438-7-4

Photography by David & Rosemary Watson

Graphics and design by Rosemary Watson

CONTENTS

INTRODUCTION

Perthshire has scores of waterfalls and cascades. This little book is designed to focus on about 20, all of which are accessible with no more than a moderate walk. There is a multitude of other falls awaiting the mountaineer and keen walker. The falls we include are all in modern-day Perthshire, except for two, which we have hi-jacked from neighbouring authorities.

How are waterfalls created?

Running through Perthshire in a south-west to northeast trend is the Highland Boundary fault, which divides highland Scotland from the lowlands. To the north are generally hard igneous and metamorphic rocks, but to the south are softer rocks such as sandstones, which erode more easily. As rivers fall over the Highland Boundary along Strathearn, they form a line of waterfalls. The Deil's Cauldron at Comrie is formed in this way. Most other falls result from glaciation. During the various ice ages the main valleys were occupied by huge glaciers, which gradually cut down to create the well-known "U-shape". But ice in the tributary valleys was effectively "dammed" by the main glaciers, and theses valleys were left "hanging" above the major glens. Streams from them had to cascade down the steepened mountain sides, and so produced waterfalls. Those at Bruar and Acharn are of this type.

The environment of the waterfall

Over the centuries sheep and deer have denuded the Highlands of trees, except in the ravines and deep valleys where we find our waterfalls. In Strathearn for example, the deeply incised valley in which we find the Deil's Cauldron is also the location of Perthshire's biggest upland oak woodland. And in the Tay valley, the famous Birks of Aberfeldy, where we find the Falls of Moness, are a wealth of all sorts of deciduous trees, not only "birks" (birches) but also oak, beech, ash and a host of smaller trees such as hazel.

The Hermitage, near Dunkeld is home to some of Britain's biggest trees, and similarly the Falls of Bruar are surrounded by coniferous plantations, especially larch. In the spring the woods around waterfalls are a mass of flowers, often covered in Bluebells and Primroses. In autumn there is also a special beauty, with some of the falls, such as Acharn, looking their best at this time.

Falls of Acharn in autumn

If it were not for the fact that Sput Rolla is under the control of Scottish Hydro Electric, it might well be one of the best known waterfalls in southern Scotland. As it is, the magnificent spectacle is switched on and off according to a timetable, and the amount of water in the Glen Lednock hydro dam.
In full flow the falls are truly magnificent, with numerous cascades falling 30-40 metres over an inclined rock slab, before tumbling in several streams into a collection of deep gashes at the base of the main fall.
Though it is difficult to get close to the falls, a good view is obtained from the principal bend in the road on the way up to the dam, where there is plenty of room to park. The road is steep, reflecting the change of slope which produces the falls 50 metres or so to the west.
Scottish Hydro Electric are able to supply dates when the falls will be in full flow.

Sput Rolla in Glen Lednock

How to get there
Grid ref: NN 728 284
Situated 500 metres below the Lednock Dam about 7.5 km (4.5 miles) north of
Comrie. The single track allows public access all the way to the dam. There are two gates on the way up. Leave them exactly as you find them.

THE DEIL'S CAULDRON
Glen Lednock

How to get there

Grid ref: NN 768 236. Located on the Lednock river as it tumbles over the Highland Boundary fault line above Comrie. Accessed either from the Glen Lednock road, or on the Deil's Cauldrom Circular Walk, which starts at the car-park as you enter Comrie from the direction of Crieff. There is a map and information board at the start of the walk.

The Deil's Cauldron (Devil's Cooking Pot), the most visited waterfall in Strathearn, occupies the deep gorge which the headward erosion of the falls has created over millions of years. If you are reasonably fit, take the circular walk, starting from the car park near the golf course at the east end of Comrie. (Grid ref: NN 777 223)

A clockwise walk takes in the falls on the way up as you travel through the woods on the west side of the River Lednock. Alternatively, an anticlockwise walk takes you up through Laggan Wood on the east side of the river, out on to open hillside below Balmuik Farm, across Shaky Bridge and then back down Monument Road, taking in the falls as you re-enter the woodland.

A well-made board-walk and steps down from the road give safe access to view the falls, which are hidden deep at the head of the gorge, where the River Lednock cascades down into a deep water-worn plunge pool, the "Deil's Cauldron".

If you would rather drive than walk, then take the road from Comrie for Glen Lednock which leaves the A85 at the Deil's Cauldron restaurant, about 200 metres on the St Fillans side of the White Church. Take the road uphill for about a mile until you are just emerging from the woods. On your right you will see parking for 2 or 3 cars. Park and walk back a short distance until you see the board walk signposted for the falls on your left.

The Wee Cauldron

Whichever route you take, the Wee Cauldron, a series of smaller and more accessible cascades, is also worth a visit. It is located roughly half way between the Deil's Cauldron and Comrie, and is on the Glen Lednock Circular Walk. As with much of this area, it is especially attractive in autumn.

BALMENOCH
(Lawers)

How to get there
Grid ref: NN 796 233. In the woods, north of Lawers House, east of Comrie, where the Balmenoch Burn plunges to the Lowlands, as it crosses the Highland Boundary Fault.
Parking is scarce on the A85, so regard this as a 2 mile round walk. Park opposite Milton (Grid ref: NN 783 224), 100 metres towards Comrie from West Lodge caravan site. Walk past the caravan site to the end of the pavement.

Cross the road and head through the wall on to a track which after 1km (0.5 miles) ends up behind Fordie Lodge. On the way you will find some spectacular redwood trees. Turn left for about 500 metres when you meet the estate road. Just before a substantial stone-built house, take the track to the right. Less than 100 metres on, after the rear gate to the house, you will cross the Balmenoch burn, then turn on to the small track to the left leading to the falls.

There are two falls, neither of them in the deep inaccessible gorge which is normal for Strathearn waterfalls. The path follows close to the burn, and the first fall, the smaller, reached in less than 200 metres, is a delightful cascade, inviting one to photograph from its base, even when in spate. Everywhere are moss-covered boulders, ferns, wild strawberries and wood sorrel.

The upper falls

The lower falls

The main falls are a few hundred metres further up the track, and although not so pretty, and difficult to photograph, are relatively unusual in allowing access directly to the base. In spate the falls are a foaming mass of water, whereas much of the time they are a fairly gentle trickle, over about 20 metres of rock. At the base the burn divides into two, one branch continuing as the Balmenoch burn and the other flowing into the small artificial loch at Lawers.

ALLT NA DROCHAIDE
(Glen Artney)

Waterfalls in Perthshire come in all sizes, and this is the smallest we shall describe.. It is also just about the most delightful, and probably the safest for children. There is parking beside the road for two or three cars.

The fall is about 50 metres from the road, and consists of a 6 metre cascade, and a delightful little rocky stream below the fall. There is a small knoll which screens a lovely place for a picnic from the road. During the summer this is the ideal place for small children to "plowter". One of Perthshire's secret, little gems.

Common plants found in shady places

How to get there
Grid ref: NN 731 172
Located next to the Glen Artney single-track road, on the south side of the glen, about 8 km (5 miles) from Comrie.

BUCHANTY SPOUT

The term "spout" refers to a waterfall where a river is squeezed through a narrow channel and is ejected at the other side. At Buchanty the whole of the River Almond is forced through a gap, little more than a metre wide, before discharging into a deep ravine which runs under the road to Harrietfield. In the autumn, with a large flow of water, this is one of Perthshire's principal salmon leaps, a place to view the magnificent Atlantic Salmon, as they battle their way upstream to their spawning grounds.

Buchanty Spout

Ancient, abandoned potholes provide evidence of former watercourses, used before the stream eroded its bed deeper into the rock. As with most waterfalls, the site is unfenced, with sheer drops into deep ravines. Care must be taken at all times, and children will require close supervision.

One of the many potholes on the rocky banks

The highly stepped rocks near the edge

How to get there
Grid ref: NN 934 283
About 2km (just over 1 mile) east of the junction of the B8063 and the A 822 (Crieff to Dunkeld road). There is a little parking place just before the bridge over the River Almond, from which a

path leads off to the Spout. Take care, as the path soon heads over uneven, highly stepped, and sometimes slippery rocks.
Not wheelchair friendly. Difficult surfaces for anyone who has any problems with walking.

How to get there

Grid ref: NN 997 411

Located at the point where a minor road crosses the River Braan, off the A822 Crieff to Dunkeld road, about 3km (2 miles) west of Dunkeld. There is parking in the woods between the A822 and the bridge, with only a short walk. It is also possible to incorporate the falls in a circular walk from Dunkeld, which is included in the Dunkeld Walls map available at Visit Scotland in the Square. Wheelchair friendly from the car park to the bridge.

deep gorge. This is the Braan's penultimate fall in its descent to join the Tay, and it can provide an impressive spectacle.

River Braan before it plunges into the gorge

As with many falls, the unfenced sections present a hazard for unsupervised children of all ages.

A place to stop on a warm summer's day

The view of the falls from the bridge

This is one of those fairly common types of waterfall where a bridge is built over the falls, just as the river plunges into a

THE FALLS OF BRAAN
at the Hermitage

FALLS OF BRAAN
The Hermitage

The falls at the Hermitage are the last on the Braan before it tumbles into the Tay. They are located in a veritable "woodland garden", created by the famous tree-planting Duke of Athol in the 19th century, and including, reputedly, the tallest tree in the UK, a Douglas Fir which presently stands at over 65 metres.

known as Ossian's Hall, through which one passes to reach a viewing gallery. The walks are truly lovely, and are very popular during the main holiday season.

The old stone bridge

The path to the Hermitage

The falls are located immediately upstream from a lovely moss-covered stone bridge, and an 18th century folly

How to get there
Grid Ref: NN 010 423
Accessed directly off the main A9 road, just north of Dunkeld where there is a National Trust for Scotland car park, for

which you must pay. There are good paths, which are wheelchair friendly until just below the falls, after which there are steps.

13

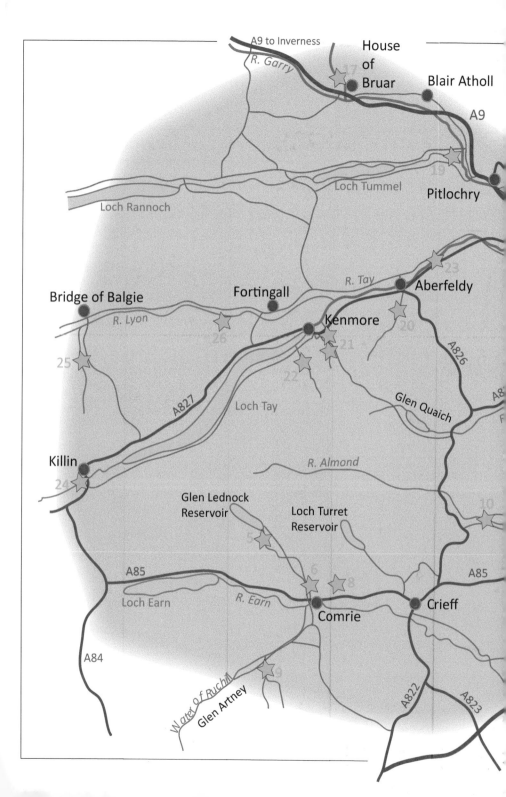

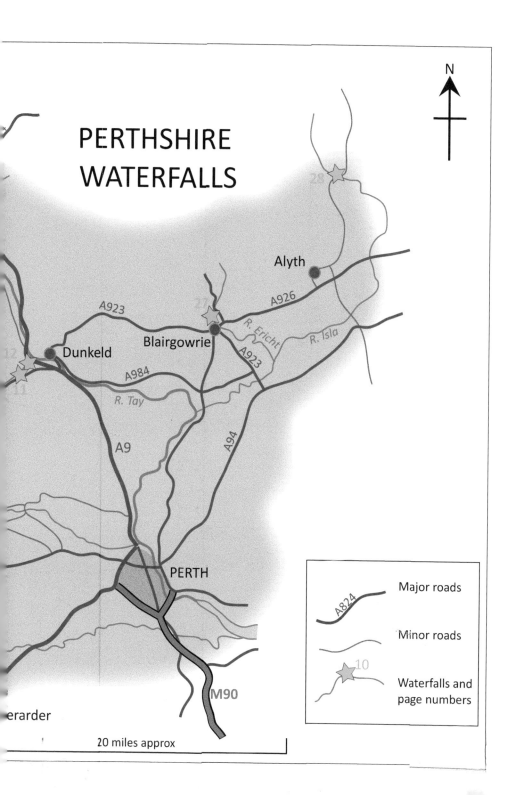

THE FALLS OF BRUAR

The Upper Falls of Bruar

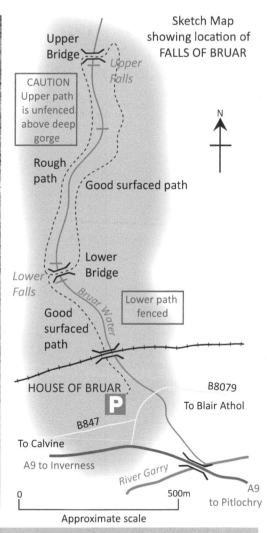

Sketch Map showing location of FALLS OF BRUAR

Upper Bridge

Upper Falls

CAUTION Upper path is unfenced above deep gorge

N

Rough path

Good surfaced path

Lower Bridge

Lower Falls

Bruar Water

Lower path fenced

Good surfaced path

HOUSE OF BRUAR

P

B8079

To Blair Athol

B847

To Calvine

A9 to Inverness

River Garry

0   500m

A9 to Pitlochry

Approximate scale

How to get there
Grid Ref: NN 822 060
Located just off the A9 at the House of Bruar, approximately 5 km (3 miles) west of Blair Athol. Access via House of Bruar complex and an excellent path network, on the west side of the burn.

The walk is about 2.0 km (just over 1 mile) round trip to Lower Falls; 4.0 km (2.5 miles) round trip to Higher Falls. Allow 1 to 2 hours depending on fitness and how long you wish to dwell in this beautiful terrain.

The Falls of Bruar are probably the most visited falls in Perthshire, perhaps even in Scotland, for many reasons. There is very good parking, all the facilities you might need, and excellent access. In comparison with some falls, there is also first class interpretive information.

The paths to the falls are in two sections. The part up to the lower bridge is the best, and gives safe views of the falls with all its cascades, potholes and amazing water-formed carvings. The section immediately above and below the lower bridge is especially outstanding. The whole of this section is very child-friendly, with a steel fence along its entire length.

As with many falls which we visit in autumn, the Falls of Bruar exhibit a superb wealth of fungi.

Some of the common fungi

The section to the upper bridge is less interesting for the waterfall watcher, but it is a nice, tough, woodland walk along the top of a steep sided gorge. This section is unfenced, and although the path on the west side of the burn is quite rough, it is always relatively safe, with lots of vegetation along the top of the gorge.

The path on the eastern side is better-surfaced, but more exposed, and would require children to be absolutely supervised, as there are very steep slopes dropping down 100 metres or more into the gorge.

View upstream from the lower bridge

The views of the upper falls are also more limited, with only one complete view of the main waterfall, from the eastern bank, looking back up the gorge towards the upper bridge. If you are taking small children, it may be best to turn round at the lower bridge.

BLACK SPOUT

How to get there

Grid ref: NN 953 576.
The usual route to Black Spout is from the road entering Pitlochry from the A9 at Grid ref: NN 950 570, where a small road passes under the railway embankment into a woodland car park and picnic site. From here a track goes uphill, along the edge of Athol Palace Hotel golf course, and after only a few hundred metres through deciduous woodland, reaches the viewing platform of this impressive fall.

One can also approach from upstream on a path which starts at the Edradour distillery. Neither routes are wheelchair friendly.

The viewing platform overlooking the falls

Black Spout is located on the Edradour burn next to Pitlochry. The falls are quite substantial, with a total height of between 50 and 60 metres, depending on who you believe. The final fall is an impressive "spout" into a deep gorge. As with the construction of numerous other viewing platforms at Perthshire's waterfalls, the work was undertaken by the army.

THIS VIEWING PLATFORM WAS PROVIDED BY THE ROTARY CLUB OF PITLOCHRY AND CONSTRUCTED BY ABERDEEN UNIVERSITY OFFICER TRAINING CORPS IN JULY 1989.

Black Spout

Also in Black Spout woods is the recently excavated Black Spout Iron Age homestead. (See Perth and Kinross Heritage Trust www. pkht.org.uk)

How to get there
Grid ref: NN 908 600
Leave the A9 from the section by-passing Pitlochry. Leave on the east side of the road on the minor road signed for "Clunie and Foss", which then passes under the main road. Continue past the impressive entrance to Clunie power-station, for a few hundred metres, to a car park on the left side of the road. A small, stepped woodland path, and a short walk to the falls is sign-posted on the right side of the road. Not wheelchair friendly.

The Linn of Tummel is the last protest of the River Tummel before it joins with the River Garry and enters Loch Faskally. Though both rivers are much used for hydro-electricity, there is more than sufficient flow on the Tummel to create an impressive little fall.
The whole area of south Loch Tummel is one of Perthshire's often undiscovered gems, with most of the traffic continuing north on the A9 or concentrating on Queen's View on the north side of the loch. This area is superb for safe and quiet picnicking, with lots of sites along the loch-side or to the south of the road

TheLinn of Tummel

19

FALLS OF MONESS

How to get there
Grid ref: NN 853 475
Best visited on one of the walks from
Trails of the Upper Tay, a walking map
available at Visit Scotland offices.
Park in the Birks of Aberfeldy car park,
which is located only 200 metres south
of the crossroads in Aberfeldy, on the
A826 road to Crieff, where there are
information boards.
Round-trip from the car park is about
3.0km (about 2.0 miles), with approximately 200 metres (600 feet) of climb-
ing. Suggested time 1-2 hours.
Not wheelchair friendly.

The Falls of Moness are at the head of
the woods made famous by Burns as
the Birks of Aberfeldy. Included in the
song is the verse:

"The braes ascend like lofty wa's
The foaming stream, deep-roaring fa's
O'er-hung wi' fragrant spreading shaws,
The birks of Aberfeldie."

From the car park the path begins a
gradual ascent through mixed woodland, mainly beech, with "birks"
(birches) becoming more prominent on
the upper slpoes of the valley. Choose
either side of the burn, with the
western side the easier ascent. The
substantial falls come into view almost
at the top of the walk, and a bridge
crosses right at the head of the waterfall.
The walk is lovely at all times of year,
but especially in the autumn.

TOMBUIE BURN

How to get there
Grid ref: NN 790 444
Drive from Kenmore on the steep and winding, single-track road for Glen Quaich and Amulree. After about 1.5km (1 mile) the road passes Tombuie Cottage, turns right and heads uphill. After about 200 metres, and a sharp bend to the left, there is a grassy parking spot on the left, enough for two or three cars. The waterfall is across the road, beyond the grove of mature larch trees.

This is another of Perthshire's little gems, a water-chute of 6-8 metres into a dark, round plunge pool, a truly delightful and fairly safe little waterfall. Sixty or seventy metres below the falls, on the same side as the road, is a flat terrace, a secluded dell, perfect for a picnic. This would be a lovely spot for a family outing.

The frozen water-chute and plunge pool

The Tombuie Burn is one of the many Perthshire streams which has a series of waterfalls, and another little "gem", and certainly the easiest to view, is just before the burn passes under the A827 (Aberfeldy-Killin road) at NN 784 454, where there is a little parking spot immediately on the Aberfeldy side of the bridge. This waterfall is especially lovely in autumn.

A lovely roadside waterfall on the A827

21

How to get there

Grid ref: NN 766 438
Park in Acharn village on the south Loch Tay road, about 2km (1.5 miles) west of Kenmore. Then proceed up the west side of the burn, a stiff climb for about 500 metres, following a farm track. The lower falls are not signed at the time of writing, and are accessed through the "hermit's cave". The upper falls are 100 metres further on, and falls and viewing platform are signed. Always stay on the paths, especially in the vicinity of the falls.
Not wheel chair or baby buggy friendly.

We made our second visit to Acharn in autumn, and at this time, without doubt, the Lower Acharn Fall is one of the most lovely in Perthshire, set as in an amphitheatre, surrounded by autumn colours, especially of beech. Access is through the rather dark and forbidding "Hermit's Cave", a T-shaped folly, built in Victorian times as an approach to the falls, leading out to a viewing platform which offers a splendid view.
The Upper Falls are another 100 metres further up the track and a viewing platform and bridge allow you to view another lovely collection of cascades and huge cauldron-like black pot-holes, which have been created by the swirling waters over thousands of years.
Take care that you keep children supervised here, especially between the track and the bridge.
There is another bridge just upstream,

this time of stone, though the view from it is not so special. However, if you cross it, is possible to return to Acharn down the right side of the burn, though the path is more difficult than the left side. Alternatively you may wish to continue up the track about 500 metres, and visit one of Scotland's best located stone circles. (See "An introduction to the Stone Circles and Standing Stones of Perthshire" by David Watson)

The lower falls of Acharn

How to get to Grandtully Rapids
Grid ref: NN 914 434.
The Rapids are right next to the road on the River Tay, upstream from the Grandtully bridge on the A837 Ballinluig to Aberfeldy road.

Though technically not strictly 'waterfalls", the rapids are well worth a visit from waterfall enthusiasts, if only because of how they are used. This is one of the principal home waters for Scottish canoeists, and on many days of the year one can see kayaks of all colours negotiating the permanent slalom course.

The response of the canoeing fraternity to the rapids is shown in their adopted names for various sections, "Zoom Flume" and "Washing Machine" give you a flavour.

Grandtully Rapids

If you are after adrenaline, white water rafting, which also takes place here, is possibly the activity for you. Trips usually start downstream from Aberfeldy and finish at Grandtully. Check out companies with Visit Scotland or google "white water rafting on the Tay", and you will find a list of suppliers.

The canoes make a colourful spectacle

The spectacle of the rapids and the bright colours of the conoes also provide a good photo-location, with the bridge over to Strathtay giving the best viewpoint.

There is also an excellent coffee shop across the road from the rapids with good coffee, lovely home baking and truly civilized toilets.

A canoeist on the rapids

FALLS OF DOCHART

How to get to the Falls of Dochart
Grid ref: NN 571 325
On the A827 road in Killin. There is parking on the south side of the bridge, or in the village. Accessible for wheelchair users, but the best viewing point, the bridge, is often busy with traffic.

Looking across the river to the Folklore Centre

The Falls of Dochart

The Falls of Dochart are about 2 kilometres outside Perth and Kinross, but as they occur on the River Dochart, the main water supply for Loch Tay, we will claim them anyway. The Dochart generally has a copious supply of water, and above the bridge, the falls split into a series of tumbling channels, as the river eventually descends to the level of Loch Tay, still about 100 metres above sea level.

These are perhaps the most visited and photographed falls in southern Scotland, and possibly the whole country. In spate, which is often, they are spectacular. At times when the water is low, access to the rocky slabs on the south side of the falls provides a relatively safe photo-opportunity or place to picnic. This being

said, as at most waterfalls, children will need close supervision.

Otherwise, the bridge is the ideal place for a picture, and in the holiday season, you will not be alone.

On the Loch Tay side of the bridge, on a little island in the river, is the Clan McNab burial ground.

The Breadalbane Folklore Centre is in the old mill across the bridge, and the delights of Killin and its main street start there also. On the south side of the bridge is the Falls of Dochart Inn, one of the best-known pubs in the area.

The entrance to Clan McNab burial ground

How to get there
Grid ref: NN677 426 and northwards for 2km. On the Allt Bail a Mhuilinn burn, a tributary of the River Lyon, between Loch Tay and Bridge of Balgie. Generally within 100 metres of the road.

Most waterfalls seem to be deeply entrenched in wooded gorges, and are therefore relatively inaccessible, but not this one, or rather more accurately this "series" of cascades. They are located on the delightful highland road which joins together Loch Tay and the upper part of Glen Lyon. The road reaches an altitude of over 500 metres and is usually best avoided in winter, but for the rest of the year it is a delight, with a host of spectacular water features.

A section of the cascades

There is a series of cascades, each dropping perhaps 30-40 metres and all gloriously visible only 50 metres or so from the road. On the lower sections, in the last two kilometres before Bridge of Balgie, as well as an official picnic and parking site with interpretive information boards, there are also numerous spots where you can pull off the road and picnic beside one of the cascades.

A picnic spot near a cascade

Combine your waterfall picnic with an ascent of Ben Lawers or Ben Ghlas. Most walkers leave from the National Trust for Scotland car park near the southern end of the Loch Tay to Bridge of Balgie road. In addition, Ben Lawers is a National Nature Reserve, with a special collection of sub-Arctic flora, and a range of alpine plants found nowhere else in UK.

25

ALLT DA GHOB
(Packhorse Bridge)

Grid ref: NN696 472.
Located on the south side of the River
Lyon, just before the Allt Da-Ghob burn
passes under an old packhorse bridge
and enters the River Lyon. There are
small spaces off-road for one or two cars
in the vicinity, amongst the beech trees,
but no proper car park.

The easiest way to find the falls is to
head into Glen Lyon on the single track
road, which heads off from the road
between Fortingall and Fearnan. After
about 3.5 km (about 2 miles) of winding
through the gorge section of the River
Lyon, an open field appears across the
river to the left, together with a private
footbridge. Continue along the road past
the bridge for a further 300 metres, and
the falls appear across the main river,
immediately behind the old packhorse
bridge.

This is one of those "picture-postcard"
locations which all waterfall photogra-
phers must have. After several unsuc-
cessful visits, we decided that it was
necessary to don serious waders before
heading out into the river.

Waders in your car may prove useful!

As decided by the Ordnance Survey, who
use an image of these falls on the cover
of Landranger Map 51, this is a delightful
little waterfall, especially in autumn,
with the juxtaposition of the falls and
the old bridge making for a special
composition. But it is devilishly difficult
to photograph, as the branches of large
beech trees sweep down over the river
to block one's views. Serious photo-
seekers should take wellie-boots, to
avoid the branches, so long as the river
is not in spate.

Packhorse Bridge, Glen Lyon

How to get there
Grid ref: NO 178 460
About 800 metres upstream from the bridge linking Blairgowrie with Rattray, and accessed from the parking and picnic area at Lower Mill Street, Blairgowrie, alongside the riverside path, just north of the bridge.

We include the falls at Blairgowrie not because they are spectacular, but because the town was long-associated with mills which were driven by falling water. The remains of many of Blairgowrie's weirs can still be seen, both above and below the falls, and at one time it is said there were thirteen of them.

One of the thirteen mills, now made into flats

The Falls of Ericht make up a series of cascades in a small gorge, where a band of sandstone runs across the course of the river. On the west side, parallel to the river, one can see the "excavations"

through the rock of a planned mill lade. At Donald Cargill's Leap, the river is confined to a narrow cascade, where the whole of the Ericht flow hurtles through only a few metres, particularly spectacular when the river is in spate.

The Ericht above Blairgowrie

Donald Cargill was a 17th century Covenanter, who is said to have fled from pursuing soldiers, by leaping across the falls at the narrowest part of the gorge. Alas, the attempts, over succeeding centuries, by Blairgowrie's youth to emulate the feat, and the damage they caused themselves, eventually caused the local council to dynamite the rocks and make the narrow gap wide enough for it to be impossible for anyone to leap it. Along the walk from the town, a number of viewing platforms have been built, and there is a footbridge above the falls giving an excellent view of upstream weirs and former mills which depended on them.

REEKIE LINN

Reekie Linn is by far the biggest and most spectacular waterfall which we include, and is formed where the River Isla is obstructed by volcanic rocks 200 metres below Craigisla Bridge.

We feel it is also necessary to mention that we feel it is also the most dangerous waterfall, with the path and various access points running along the top of an unfenced gorge, with a drop of about 45 metres (150 feet). Certainly not a place for unsupervised children.

Having said that, the falls are spectacular, especially after heavy rain, when the mist from the falls creates the sensation of smoke, hence "Reekie" Linn. If you are lucky, especially on a sunny morning, you might get a rainbow in the mist.

The fall drops perhaps 30 metres (100 feet), in two steps, which merge into one when the river is in spate, and probably has no competitors in southern Scotland. It is, quite simply, majestic.

Reekie Linn with its rainbow on a sunny day

Grid Ref: NO 254 537

Located immediately on the east side of Bridge of Craigisla, where there is a car park and picnic spot with benches. Reekie Linn is technically in Angus, but as it is just over the border, and is so spectacular, we have decided to claim it for Perthshire, just for this little book.